POEMS
FOR
THE
CAT

Author

Brian Daniel Starr

POEMS FOR THE CAT

ISBN-13:
978-1495268762

ISBN-10:
1495268764

Printed in the United States of America

DEDICATION

To

Lovely Daughter

Gabriella Maria

Starr

And My Loving Fiancée Lindsay Anne

Who have given me the Patience and fortitude to Complete this work

Also Dedicated to the cause for

Sainthood for

Blessed Venerable Servant of
God

Pope John Paul II

and

Venerable Servant of God

Father Michael McGivney

Founder of the Knights of
Columbus

Table of Contents

DEDICATION 4

THE GREAT SIMBA 9

BENGALI 11

ROY 12

OZ 13

CHEETAH 14

BOB 15

HOUSE 16

PRIDE..19

MOTHER CAT 21

TOMCAT 22

TOM AND JERRY 23

FAMOUS CAT 24

CAT THAT NEEDS KEEPING 26

ANIMAL CATS 27

CAT FIGHT..30

CLEAN CAT 31

RESTING CAT 32

THE GREAT SIMBA

GREAT KING OF THE BEASTS

TELL YOUR WIFE TO GO FETCH THE
FOOD

ROAR YOUR GREAT ROAR SO ALL
BEASTS KNOW YOU ARE KING

GREAT LION SESOTKIS KAUPERRE

WHO IS GREATER THAN THOU

WATCH YOUR PRIDE OF SINBA'S TAKE
THE LARGE PINAJEB MACCABEE OLLIE
THE ELEPHANT COW

FEAST ON THE FLESH

FOR WHO CAN KILL YOU IN HAND TO
HAND

NONE SAVE THE MAN

AND IS MAN NOT FAR AWAY

MAKE MAN PAY WITH YOUR CLAWS
AND YOUR TEETH BEFORE YOUR NOBLE
JAW IS BROKEN AND YOUR HEART
FOOD FOR THE DANITE

FOR EVEN YOU SIMBA, HAS HIS MASTER

BENGALI

IN INDIA DO YOU LIVE WELL ON
NATIVE FLESH OF MAN

BENGALI IS A FIRE STICK YOUR ONLY
ENEMY

AND WHO COULD FIGHT YOU IN HAND
TO HAND

WHY DO YOU FEAST ON THE NATIVE
MAN

IS THE SONS OF ISHBACK EASY PREY
FOR YOUR LARGE APPETITE BENGALI

WHAT MAKES THE DANITE YOUR
FRIEND IN HAND TO HAND

DO YOU CRAVE THE DEATH OF MAN OR
OF THE DANITE YOUR MASTER

ROY

ORPHAN OF FORTUNE

IS A GOOD WAY TO TAME BENGALI IN
THE CAGE

AND WHAT FAIR KNIGHT PROVOKES THE
DOM OF THE TIGER

TO HAVE YOU EATEN THAT DAY

AND WHO CARES AS MADONNA AND
DAN RULE THE SUBCONCIOUS AS YOU
RECOVER

FOR WHO CARES FOR THE ORPHAN MAN
IN THE HOSPITAL

IS NOT HIS LIFE LIVED LONG ENOUGH

AT THE STATE FAIR IS THE OFFERING
TO LET THE ALBINO TIGER EAT THE
TAMER

FOR WHO ELSE CAN REFUSE JOSHUA
BUT DAN

SO THE BAMBOO REMAINS THE TIGERS
ONLY FOOD THAT DAY

LONG LIVE THE BENGALI TAMER

OZ

LIONS AND TIGERS AND BEARS OH MY

LIONS AND TIGERS AND BEARS OH MY

LIONS AND TIGERS AND BEARS OH MY

.

LISTEN MOM TELL KING JAMES I CAN
ERASE THE DOT

IT'S LIONS AND TIGERS AND LEOPARDS
IN NICOLES BLOOD OF HANNITY

WHO CAN TEACH A DOG NEW TRICKS

A CAT

CHEETAH

HOW FAST ARE YOU

ARE YOU THE DESIGN OF THE YEAR

FOR ADAM MAKES HIS LIVING
DESIGNING ANIMALS FOR HIS DAD

AND LOOK AT THAT BOY WAS HE
DRUNK THAT DAY

BUT WHEN HE THOUGHT ABOUT THE
CHEETAH

HOW FAST AND SLEEK

ACCELERATION, TURN ON A DIME, AND
RUN DOWN THE FAST FOUR LEGGED
ANTELOPE

SCARED TO DEATH FOR THEIR LIFE

LEAPING 25 FEET FOR THE CHEETAH
TO SINK HIS TEETH INTO THE THROAT

AND EAT THE FLESH

BOB

WHO ARE YOU BOB

SMALL FURRY AND WILD

A CAT THAT CAN CLIMB

EATS SMALL PREY

DOGS STAY AWAY

AND THE GROWL NOT AS LOUD

AS SIMBA OR BENGALI

BUT STILL A SCARE FOR MAN TO
SHARE

IF MET IN THE MOUNTAIN

THE BOBCAT WILL RUN FROM THE
HERMIT

HOUSE

CAT IN THE HOUSE

DO NOT GO STRAY

FOR WHEN I FEEL ANGER

YOU ARE THERE TO PLAY

INSIST ON MY PET

WHEN YOU WANT NOT I

YET YOU DO KNOW THE WAY

INTO THE CAGE WHEN THE LAW

OF MAN TELLS YOU SO

FOR PET THOU YOU SEEM

TO YOU MAN IS PREY

FOR A CAT DOESN'T KNOW

IF IT'S DAN OR A MAN

YOUR CLAWS STAY SHARP

AND YOUR FOOD YOU DO EAT

TRAINED NOT IN THE LITTER

YOU KEEP YOURSELF CLEAN

AND WHEN DO YOU GO OFF

WHEN YOU ARE TRAPPED BY YOUR
FOLLY

FOR A HOUSE CAT YOU ARE

A PET MOST IMPRESSED

TO HIDE FROM YOUR MAN

WHEN YOU SEE

AND WHAT DO YOU SEE

HOW COMPLICATED ARE YOU

FOR YOUR EYES HAVE A SHINE

AND A LOVE THAT IS REAL

A FAMILIAR FOR SOME

BUT A CAT SO IDEAL

THAT LOVE FOR THE BEAST

IS JUST YOU THERE AT PLAY

AND FAITHFUL YOU UNDERSTAND

IS NOT WHAT YOU PLAY

FOR IS NOT MAN TO FEED

AND CLEAN AND BE

YOUR SERVANT FOR YOU ARE THE
KING OF THE BEASTS

IN THE HOUSE KEPT WARM AND DRY

FOR YOU MY DEAR CAT

MY FIRST PET I CAN HAVE

FOR WOMEN NOT MET

AN ALLERGY FOR YOU

FOR ARE YOU NOT THE PET FOR ME

YOUR SERVANT FOR YOU ARE THE
KING OF THE BEASTS

IN THE HOUSE KEPT WARM AND DRY

FOR YOU MY DEAR CAT

PRIDE

HOW BIG IS THE PRIDE OF THE CAT

FOR WHAT IS THE NAME

OF THE TABBY YOU FIND

A HUMAN NAME THAT YOU BEAR

OR IS YOUR NAME SACRED

TO THOSE WHO WOULD WORSHIP

THE DARK OF THE BLACK

AND THE WAY OF THE WICKED

IS YOUR COAT BLACK SO THAT ON
HALLOWEEN

YOUR LIFE IS A SACRIFICE TO THE
WITCH THAT IS MEAN

OH TABBY SO NICE

LICK ON MY FLESH FOR YOU NEED THE
SALT THAT IS ON MY SKIN

AND REMEMBER NOT THE DAY

THAT FATEFUL DAY WHEN THE CAR
THAT I DROVE MET YOUR BODY SO
DEAR

DID YOU MAKE IT MY FRIEND FROM
THE VET THAT YOU MET

OR WAS IT DEATH BY MECHANICAL
DEVICE

POOR TABBY MY FRIEND SO FAST IN
THE DART

UNDER THE WHEELS SO THE PIZZA IS
THERE IN THE TIME THAT WAS SAID

OR PAY NOT THE MAN A PIECE OF
MAN IT IS SAID

FOR THE CAT THAT WOULD DART
UNDER THE MECHANICAL CART

WOULD FORGIVE THE MAN

WHO CAN'T DRIVE WORTH A DAMN

IT WAS THE CAR MY FRIEND NOT I

MOTHER CAT

HOW MANY YOU HAVE

KITTENS GALORE

FOR A CAT WITH A MATE

WILL MAKE MANY MORE

AND HOW WILL YOU LIVE

EATING SMALL PREY LIKE MICE

FOR MOTHER CAT KNOWS

SHE IS BIGGER THAN SOME

TOMCAT

WHAT IS THE TOMCAT

A STROKE IN THE DARK?

PETTING SO HARD

BUT ONLY WHERE WE ARE ALLOWED

SHOULD WE KEEP CLEAN

OR NO NOT THAT

FOR THE TOMCAT

IS A VIRGIN ONLY ONCE

TOM AND JERRY

IS PEPI LA PEW A CAT?

IS THE TOM YOUR WAY?

WHAT ABOUT WATER AND THIRST?

CAN A CAT EAT A FISH?

NOT IF THE FISH IS IN WATER.

IS JERRY A FROG?

MOST MAGNIFICENT PREDITOR

CAT MOST FEROUCIOUS

OWN PAUL AND ELEVEN TRIBES

BUT OWN NOT YOUR PHAROAH

FAMOUS CAT

WHO IS THE CAT OF FAME

WHAT CAT COMES TO MIND

FOR ME IT IS CAT WOMEN

AND BATMAN MUST KNOW

THAT THE CAT OF THE CHASE

WILL WIN EVERY TIME

FOR CATWOMEN CAN WIGGLE AS THE
FAMOUS CAT CAN

AND BOY ROBIN MUST WONDER

WHAT REALLY HAPPENS IN THE BAT
CAVE

WHEN POOR BATMAN IS CAPTURED BY

HIS MATE OF HIS RHYME

FOR IS THE CAT THE BAT OR THE BAT
THE CAT

A SPANK HERE AND THERE

FOR THE BLOOD OF THE BAT

AND THE BLOOD OF THE CAT

MUST KEEP THE YOUNG ROBIN INNOCENT

MUST KEEP THE YOUNG ROBIN INNOCENT

CAT THAT NEEDS KEEPING

EVERY CAT THAT WE KNOW

MUST ONE DAY BEAR

A NEW CAT TO BE KEPT

BY THE NEED OF HER CARE

FOR EVERY BAT KNOWS

IT IS FOR THE CAT TO DECIDE

AND WHO IS TO SAY

WHO IS PICKED UP AT THE BAR

FOR SHE WILL ALLOW

THE BAT TO BUY

ALL THE POTION OF LOVE FOR THE

CAT TO GO MEOW

BUT WHEN IT IS DONE

WHO IS TO KNOW

THAT SHE ALREADY WON

AND SHE DOES NOT STAY

FOR NO CAT CAN FOLLOW ANY BUT
HER WAY

ANIMAL CATS

CHEETAH

BOB

SIMBA

BENGALI

TABBY

ALL OF YOU

THE SAME HOUSE YOU SHARE

AND NUMBER SO GREAT

A LOVE DO YOU SHARE

WITH MAN WHO CAN CONQUER

EACH ONE AT A TIME

FOR HE LOVES YOU A FRIEND

A FRIEND FOR ALL TIME

NOT A WIFE OR CHILD

AN ANIMAL TO KEEP

WHO SERVES IN A WAY

THAT IS GOOD TO KEEP

A SIMPLE SMALL THING

THAT ONLY LADY ANNE DOES KNOW

FOR TO TELL HER SHES GREAT

IS FOR HER TO KNOW

FOR SHE REALLY IS AND CATS DO YOU
KNOW

THAT TO HER BELONGS

THE WINGS OF YOUR BACK

A CREATURE DIVINE

IN THE DARK DO YOU HIDE

DINGBAT OF THE KING

WITH THE CAT FACE AND THE WINGS

OF THE CREATURE

LIKE THE BAT, THE OWL, THE EAGLE
AND THE DOVE

YOURS LADY ANNE GETS HELP FROM
ABOVE

FOR ONLY TO THE BAT AND THE
PIGEON

WITH THE OWL THERE TO GUARD

WITH THE BASTARD HAWK TO CLIMB

THE SKIES WITH THE LARK

WINGED CREATURES FROM HEAVEN
WILL HELP COME FROM THE DARK

WHILE FATE THE GREAT ANNA

MAN THAT HE IS

WILL GUARD THE TRUE LIGHT

AND THE DARK OH TO FEAR

HOW CAN WE FALL

INTO WHAT PIT OF FEAR

AND CONTEST WE MUST

THE MOST MARTYRS TO KILL

ANNES FATHERS HIS PLEDGES

SO THAT SOMEDAY

WE CAN ALL FIND

WINGED CREATURES OF HEAVEN

WHILE THE SERPENT OF BAR

KEEPS WATCH ON HIS CREATURES

THAT CAN GROW LEGS

CAT FIGHT

WHO WILL WIN SINBA BIG OR SINBA
SMALL

FOR THE PRIDE HAS IT'S RANK

AND SIMBA IS ONE ALONE

WHY CANNOT JUST ONE SINBA RULE

WHO IS THE STRONGEST FOR SIMBA

SIMBA NEEDS MANY TO MAKE THE
ELEPHANT HIS PRIZE

THE WATER HOLE IS GUARDED

DOES SIMBA CARE ?

CLEAN CAT

HOW DOES THE DANDER

OF THE CAT BOTHER SO MANY

AND IS A BATH A WAY TO KEEP
CLEAN

TOTAL SUBMERSION IS FINE

BUT THE LICK OF THE CAT

KEEPS HER CLEAN

RESTING CAT

HOW DO YOU REST CAT

WITH ONE EYE OPEN

DAMN RIGHT THERE MIGHT BE A
DEMON

OR A LARGER CAT OR A SNAKE

OR A MOUSE MIGHT BE OUT

FOR YOU TO POUNCE AND EAT

FOR THE PREDITOR NEVER SLEEPS

AND AS EACH WEAK POINT IS KNOWN

THE PREDITOR STENGTHENS THE
DEFENSE